The Memoirs of the Year 2008

GEORGE P. FERNANDEZ

iUniverse, Inc.
New York Bloomington

The Memoirs of the Year 2008

iUniverse books may be ordered through booksellers or by contacting:

iUniverse
1663 Liberty Drive
Bloomington, IN 47403
www.iuniverse.com
1-800-Authors (1-800-288-4677)

ISBN: 978-1-4401-9072-8 (pbk)
ISBN: 978-1-4401-9073-5 (ebk)

Library of Congress Control Number: 2009912063

Printed in the United States of America

iUniverse rev. date: 11/23/2009

To the memory of my parents.

Contents

Preface

This book is a personal memoir in which the author describes current events and expresses his personal reflections.

Two major events of historical importance that took place in the year 2008 are briefly mentioned in this book: the financial crisis that spread across the world and the election of Mr. Barack Obama, an African=American, as the forty-fourth president of the United States.

The grave collapse of Wall Street and its worldwide consequences was unexpected and very difficult to predict. Therefore, the "Black Swan" Theory may be applied to this event. Mr. Nassim Nicholas Taleb, a specialist in financial derivatives, an epistemologist, and a scholar of randomness, goes into this topic in his book "*The Black Swan: The Impact of the Highly Improbable*." I also deal the problem of the unforeseen in the story "The Bay of Pigs Invasion and The Imponderable" although I was unaware at that time of Mr. Taleb's book. These are two examples of illogical or even chaotic events.

It was my wish to write a personal testimony of a remarkable year.

George P. Fernandez

Miami Beach, Florida

PART ONE
Winter 2008

Thursday, January 17, 2008

Space

Space, in this case, is one of the three elements of the physical world. The other two are, as any high school student knows, velocity and time thus the equation $S = V \times T$. However I'm not here to talk about physics, this is really for a way to start this book about a world that's not always very rational with a very rational subject.

Irrationality and chaos sometimes prevails over logic and order. Maybe this is the result of struggle, or "the struggle for existence" from Charles Darwin's perspective. It may be the result of nature's need "to alter and change" as the Greek philosopher Heraclitus of Ephesus said. Heraclitus believed in war. "We must know," Heraclitus said, "that war is common to all and strife is justice, and that all things come into being and pass away through strife"-(1). My hopes are for peace.

(1.) "*A History of Western Philosophy*" by Bertrand Russell. Book-of-the-Month Club, 1995, page 42.

Saturday, January 19, 2008

Bobby Fischer

Bobby Fischer passed away last Thursday, January 17, in Reykjavik, Iceland, in the same city where he took his name to new heights thirty-six years ago in the chess world. After a long illness he died of kidney failure. He was sixty-four years old, the same number of squares on a chessboard. He is considered to be one of the greatest chess players in the history of the sport.

Dr. Max Euwe wrote in *Bobby Fischer - The Greatest?* (1979) that "it is much more interesting to compare Fischer with Lasker, Capablanca, and Alekhine than with some of the living ex-world champions who have played with Fischer over the board." (Gary Kasparov had not yet appeared in the chess world at the time of the publication of Euwe's book.)

Fischer's personality was sometimes unconventional bordering on paranoia. It seems that he was not raised properly by his mother, and he was later a high school dropout. These facts may explain his outbursts and sometimes abnormal behavior later in his life.

Bobby Fischer = Rest in peace
1943 - 2008

Saturday, January 26, 2008

Chess for Blood and Chess for Money

One of the strongest chess tournaments in the world is being played now in Wijk aan Zee, Holland, the Corus Chess Tournament. The best chess players of the world are present in this small Dutch town which is on the North Sea.

In round eleven, there was a strong battle of the minds between the Norwegian wunderkind Magnus Carlsen and the Indian Vishy Anand, who is the present world champion. The lad from Norway, playing White, launched a piercing attack on the king side of the chessboard against the Black king. Although Anand already had the king barricaded his defenses had begun to crumble before the sharp attack. Magnus, on his part, lost ground in his attack and Anand was able to move away his king. Finally the skillful Indian champion won this game by a hair.

This was a game of chess for blood and, of course, for money.

Night and Day

There is a street in Miami Beach that never sleeps. It is a street where the food is plentiful and the music either joyful or romantic mixes with the noises of the vehicles in the background. A singer intones his verses while at some distance the ocean murmurs. The street is alive. It is Ocean Drive.

Friday, February 1, 2008

A Murder on Ocean Drive

There is an article by Tania Valdemoro in the February 1 edition of the *Miami Herald* titled "Grim Walk: Versace Murder Tour Offered." It is about "a two hour walking tour of South Beach devoted to the life and murder of Versace, . . ."

Life has a dark side epidemics, devastating wars, natural catastrophes. Ocean Drive, in South Beach, had its dark moment more than ten years ago. On July 15, 1997, I was in my apartment when somebody told me that the Italian fashion designer Gianni Versace was murdered just half block away. The news about his murder went immediately around the world.

Tourists stand today in front of what was Versace's palazzo, Casa Casuarina, as he renamed the Amsterdam Palace apartments built in 1930. They may take some pictures of the building and then go walking on Ocean Drive.

Wednesday, February 6, 2008

National Politics

In the primary elections of the major political parties, the Republicans and Democrats, nothing has been settled yet. The struggle continues for the presidential race. Senator John Mc-Cain is a little ahead in the Republican party. Democratic Senators Hillary Rodham Clinton and Barack Obama are still in a tight race.

Economy

The stock market plunged yesterday by almost 3 percent due to fears that the United States economy is on the threshold of a recession. The Asian stock markets also fell sharply for the same reason and I assume the Europeans markets also fell. Don't forget that the U.S. economy, like a buoy, will always resurface. Our country has the strongest economy in the world.

Family Anecdote

In the 1920's my grandfather Juan Fernandez Jaren was a doctor in a government insane asylum in Havana. He used to sit, at lunch time, with his patients in the dining room of the hospital. One day a patient stared directly into the eyes of another patient sitting across the dining table and suddenly grabbed his plate, food and all, and threw it at the other man. The other patient did the same thing to him and then a full-fledged food fight ensued among the inmates. Guards of the hospital came in and restored order. Sometime later my grandfather resigned. He didn't like psychiatry anymore.

This is a true story.

Monday, February 11, 2008

National Politics

Senator Barack Obama already has the lead in the Democratic presidential race. Will he be able to keep this advantage? In the Republican party, Senator John Mc-Cain is, so far, the leader in the race for the nomination.

History

On February 16, 1945, President Franklin Roosevelt, British Prime Minister Winston Churchill and Soviet leader Josef Stalin signed the Yalta Agreement during World War II.-Roosevelt and Churchill asked Stalin to invite Pope Pius XII to this meeting. The Communist dictator gave them his famous answer, "How many [army] divisions does the Pope have?"

On February 15, 1898, the U.S.S. *Maine* blew up inexplicably in Havana Harbor killing 260 crew members and creating tensions between the United States and Spain. The new "yellow press" of the United States created a strong sentiment among the American people against Spain. President McKinley finally decided to declare war against Spain to begin the Spanish-American War. A treaty of peace was signed at Paris on December 10, 1898, between both countries. Spain, the defeated country, lost its last two colonies in the Americas, Cuba and Puerto Rico, and the United States was established as a world power.

Theater

Tennessee Williams passed away on February 25, 1983, in New York. On June 15, 1982, his work *A House Not Meant To Stand* was performed in the Guzman Cultural Center, Miami. The Belgian born director Andre Ernot said that this work is "a haunting comedy exploring the dreams and confusions of a troubled Mississippi family." This was the last play written by Tennessee Williams.

Health

An article written by Gina Kolata in the *New York Times*, February 12, says that "scientists are reporting that they have determined why muscles get tired and devised, for mice, an experimental drug that can eliminate fatigue." I ask myself, is it well-advised to eliminate fatigue? Sometimes I enjoy being lazy and having a long, restful night's sleep.

The Hippocratic Oath

Florida has one of the highest rates of medical malpractice lawsuits in the nation. To err is human but to make mistake because of a lack of responsibility, carelessness or, worse, for profit is regrettable. Doctors and dentists worldwide have a code of ethics.

Hippocrates was a Greek physician born in 460 B.C. on the island of Cos, Greece. He was considered to be the best physician of his time. Rejecting superstitions he treated illness based on observation and the study of the body.

In the Western world the Hippocratic Oath has been traditionally taken by physicians although it is not always obligatory. A modern version is being used today, and many American medical schools use alternatives pledges.

A modern translation of the oath[1] runs as follows:

> "I swear by Apollo Physician and Asclepius and Hygeia and Panaceia and all the gods, and goddesses, making them my witnesses, that I will fulfill according to my ability and judgment this oath and this covenant:

> To hold him who has taught me this art as equal to my parents and to live my life in partnership with him, and if he is in need of money to give him a share of mine, and to regard his offspring as equal to my brothers in male lineage and to teach them this art—if they desire to learn it—without fee and covenant; to give a share of precepts and oral instruction and all the other learning to my sons and to the sons of him who was instructed me and to pupils who have signed the covenant and have taken an oath according to the medical law, but no one else.

> I will apply dietetic measures for the benefit of the sick according to my ability and judgment; I will keep them from harm and injustice.

> I will neither give a deadly drug to anybody who asked for it, nor will I make a suggestion to this effect. Similarly I will not give to a woman an abortive remedy. In purity and holiness I will guard my life and my art.

I will not use the knife, not even on sufferers from stone, but will withdraw in favor of such men as are engaged in this work.

Whatever houses I may visit, I will come for the benefit of the sick, remaining free of all intentional injustices, of all mischief and in particular of sexual relations with both female and male persons, be they free or slaves.

What I may see or hear in the course of the treatment or even outside of the treatment in regard to the life of men, which on no account one must spread abroad, I will keep to myself, holding such things shameful to be spoken about.

If I fulfill this oath and do not violate it, may it be granted to me to enjoy life and art, being honored with fame among all men for all time to come; if I transgress it and swear falsely, may the opposite of all this be my lot."

1. Wikipedia, s.v. Hippocratic Oath.

Monday, February 18, 2008

The Gutenberg Age and The Digital Age

I have on my desk a computer and connected to it, like an appendage, the printer that I only use when necessary. I no longer sit in front of a typewriter for writing a letter instead I send an e-mail. For me the printer takes second place as a medium of communication. The digital form has in many ways displaced the printed text.⁻

The Information Superhighway is the ideal means for sending messages instantly. Billions of e-mail messages are sent everyday in a non=physical space called cyberspace.

One of the negative effects of this technological revolution is that impairs language. For example, the skill to write personal letters to parents, children, and friends is lost to a great extent. The epistle is going to be a relic of the past. The human factor has also to be considered. The e-mail lacks ⁼the intimate conversation-" found in a written letter.

We are witnesses of a period of transition in communication.

National Politics

Ohio has lost one million jobs due to NAFTA which Senator Hillary Clinton called one of "Bill's successes" and "legislative victories." This issue created a verbal dispute between Senator Barack Obama and former First Lady Hillary Clinton.

Monday, February 25, 2008

The Book in the Digital Age

Gutenberg's invention of the printer in the fifteenth century began a revolution in writing. Books were no longer written by hand on parchments by monks in monasteries instead they were printed on papers. The printed sheets allowed books to be published in series. Eventually private libraries began to appear. Reading and knowledge were no longer the monopoly of the Church.

The predominance of the bound book has lasted until recently. Computer science and new information technologies are changing the way we learn from and communicate with each other. The Internet has become the ideal medium of communication.

In his book *The Gutenberg Elegies*, American essayist and literary critic Sven Birkerts asks "What is the place of reading, and of the reading sensibility, in our [digital] culture as it has become? I think that the importance of the printed text is as solid as ever within the frame of the new information technologies. One reason is that the durability of the paper is unmatched, so far, by any electronic device. Therefore, reading literature will eventually recover most of its importance after the present high tide of high-tech culture recedes.

I have in my living room a print of the painting *A Young Girl Reading*, which was painted in 1776 by French painter Fragonard. While I look at it I think of how that was a times when reading was an enjoyment for the educated person.

National Politics

After winning the last ten Democratic presidential races Senator Barack Obama is preparing for another showdown with Senator Hillary R. Clinton in Dallas, Texas. So far Mr. Obama has been like an unstoppable locomotive running at full speed.

Monday, March 10, 2008

Spring

"Come, gentle Spring! Ethereal mildness, come."

James Thomson
1700---1748.

Chess

The Morelia (Mexico)---Linares (Spain) chess super-tournament in Spain finished on March 7. La crème de la crème of the world's chess players participated.

The winner was world champion Viswanthan Anand from India. Second place went to Magnus Carlsen, the wunderkind from Norway. And third place belonged to GM Levon Aronian from Armenia.

Ms. Nadja Woisin, reporter for ChessBase News, Hamburg, Germany.

South Beach Festival

Ocean Drive was the setting February 21 to February 24 of the South Beach Wine and Food Festival.

It is a remarkable event where many tourists come to enjoy not only the nice weather and the beach but also nice food and the best wines.

Bon appétit!

Monday, March 17, 2008

The City and the World

Calle Ocho Street Festival

This is the biggest Hispanic festival in the United States. It takes place on Southwest Eighth Street in Miami, Florida. It is estimated that more than one million people turned up to the twenty-third anniversary of this twenty-three-blocks street party. From conga lines to dancing to salsa music everybody enjoyed this festival. Latin American food was plentiful: Caribbean, Central American and South American dishes satisfied all tastes.

There was a small controversy between the Catholic Church of Miami and the organizers of this event. The Church complained that the festival should not be celebrated on Palm Sunday, being the beginning of the Holy Week. However it took place as schedule.

Economy

The weakness in the American economy rumbles the world's stock markets.

International

Political Crisis at the Top of the World

Tibet is an autonomous region and the highest geographical area of the world. It was a powerful Buddhist kingdom in the seventh and eighth centuries A.D.

Since the 1950's it has been under China's political control. The Dalai Lama, Tibet's religious leader, lives in exile in India.

PART TWO
Spring 2008

Monday, April 7, 2008

Flashes on the Horizon

Quote of the Day

"The cost of living is going up and the chance of living is going down."
Flip Wilson.

Economy

Mr. Ben S. Bernanke, the Federal Reserve chairman, expressed his concern that the American economy will be in a recession in the first half of 2008 before the Joint Economic Committee of the Congress.

In other news the unemployment rate is rising and this will strain more the personal budgets of the American people. "Friday's awful news of 80,000 lost jobs in March surprised economic forecasters who had not expected such a severe [economic] contraction," the *New York Times* reported.

Monday, April 14, 2008

The Bay of Pigs Invasion and The Imponderable

In the early 1950's I was living with my family a few blocks away from the Almendares River in the city of Marianao, Cuba. Our house was a two story building, long and narrow, and located on Columbia Boulevard. My parents rented the ground floor. It had two big bedrooms and between which was a bathroom. The dining room and the kitchen were at the end. Beyond the kitchen the end of the house, like an annex, there was a room with a bathroom for the maid. You could only go to this room by using an outside corridor connected to the kitchen. The maid never lived there so I used it as a studio for reading.

One day I was reading a book and putting it aside I lowered my head a little to think. After a while I saw myself rising from the armchair, walking out of the room, and taking the corridor all the way to the other end of the house. Standing there I looked out at a wilderness lot just behind my home and at the two mansions at each side of the lot. Then I looked far in the distance and I realized that I could see all objects very clearly. Looking to the sky I saw some black dots moving in my direction. As they got closer I realized that they were warplanes flying inland. After a while the warplanes came back, some of them dogfighting, and the remaining planes flew off to the horizon. I followed them with my eyes until they disappeared. I fixed my eyes again deep in the distance, and then I saw the sea and several gray warships.

Somebody touched my arm, I raised my head and saw the maid with a small cup of just brewed Cuban coffee. I told her what I just saw. She told me, while smiling, "Cuba is a very small country that never can be involved in such a war with another country. You were dreaming and better stop watching war movies in the theater." I laughed and agreed with her. Plain people have a common sense that some of us ignore.

On Saturday, April 15, 1961, I was standing in the living room of my home in Miramar when Mrs. Humbelina Sanchez, a friend of my family, called me from the sidewalk very excited. Once I met her there she told me to look to the sky. I saw a twin-engine warplane flying very slowly to the sea. A plume of smoke came out of its tail. I told myself "Go faster, faster …—." The news on the radio was controlled by Fidel Castro's government so we relied on rumors for news. The military air base Campo Libertad, not too far from my home, was attacked by two B-26 bombers flown by Cuban exiles. The base reported extensive damage as well as casualties among government soldiers. Two other military bases were also attacked in other parts of the island. We were told that these aerial attacks were a prelude to a land invasion.

As these attacks happened, tens of thousands of people were rounded up by government security forces. Military trucks were seen often in Fifth Avenue, and Czech-made four-barrel antiaircraft guns were placed in strategic places in the city.

On Monday, April 17, we heard that there was a landing by Cuban exiles' expeditionary forces in the Bay of Pigs. There was intense fighting between the militia and the invaders. I went to work that day and to the bank as usual. We received bad news the following day: the expeditionary forces were retreating back to the beach, all their ammunition had been expended, and they were not going to receive any military support from outside. A few days later the defeat of the invaders was complete. At my job I had to quietly stand the sarcastic jokes of the Communists.

The Cuban Missile Crisis started on October 22 of the following year and "it is often regarded as the moment in which the Cold War came closest to escalating into a nuclear war."

Looking back to those days I still ask myself how it was possible that a country as small as Cuba could be involved in such a war with another country.

Monday, April 21, 2008

Papal Visit to the United States of America

His Holiness Pope Benedict XVI arrived in the United States last Tuesday, April 15, for a six-day apostolic visit.

He had already met with some victims of sexual abuse at the hands of pedophile priests. The pope and the victims of sexual abuse, whose lives have been traumatized forever, discussed this thorny and shameful issue for the Church with sincerity and courage. In the legions of clergy there have always been a few to go astray. However the large majority of the clergy remain faithful to their vows of celibacy and obedience. But this was a tragic case since it involved children who unable to protect themselves. The pope has referred publicly in this trip to this tragic issue four times and has made it "the defining theme of his six-day visit."

The pope also mentioned the issue of illegal immigrants in the United States. The ethnic diversity of the United States is reflected in American Catholicism where Hispanic membership is growing. The illegal immigrants should be given an opportunity to legalize their status in this country, according to church officials. Their deportation, which often breaks up families, is not always fair. It is important to protect their family units and to respect their human rights. A visit to Ground Zero was also on the pope's busy schedule.

The main purpose of Pope Benedict XVI's visit to the United States was his speech at the United Nations. The Universal Declaration of Human Rights was adopted by the United Nations General Assembly sixty years ago at Palais de Chaillot, Paris and the pope argued in the general assembly was that "the promotion of human rights remains the most effective strategy for eliminating inequalities between countries and social groups, and for increasing security." The pope also said that "the will of the wider international community was being dominated by that of a few powers." He argued that the UN should be the "moral center" of world affairs. He made his opinion clear about the value of human rights and the standing of the United Nations.

Saint Thomas Aquinas (1225=1274) stated that natural law was one form of the divine reason, and that human law was only legitimate as long it harmonized with the natural law. This principle later evolved into natural rights as Catholic philosopher Jacques Maritain asserted although there are some disagreements with this conclusion. This is the basis for Pope Benedict XVI's interest in human rights on the sixtieth anniversary of the Universal Declaration of Human Rights in the United Nations.

Monday, April 28, 2008

The Internet and the Fourth Amendment

There has recently been a debate in the House Judiciary Committee's antitrust task force about "Net neutrality." The committee has discussed how much control Internet service providers should have over the information that computer users send and receive over the Internet. For quite a time "cookies" have been used to track everything you do online sometimes with the purpose of knowing your behavior. They are spying on us. This information is sometimes given to companies that advertise in the Internet. This technique, called *behavioral targeting* should be considered to be an invasion of privacy.

Network providers can also interfere with your activities on the Internet by blocking some Web sites for some of their subscribers or slowing and blocking some applications. With new technologies they may become the gatekeepers and toll collectors of the Internet.

An article on BBC News's Web site by Darren Waters titled "Stark Warning for Internet Future" in which Professor Jonathan Zittrain, professor of Internet governance and regulation at Oxford University, warns that "the future [of the Net] is potentially bleak."

Monday, May 5, 2008

The Islamic State and the Western Secular State

The Vatican newspaper *L'Osservatore Romano* said recently that "for the first time in history, we [Roman Catholics] are no longer at the top: Muslims have overtaken us." Monsignor Vittorio Formenti said that Roman Catholics account for 17.4 percent of the world population while Muslims are at 19.2 percent. Monsignor Formenti added that Muslim married couples have many children whereas Christian families are having fewer and fewer. Islam is the religion that is now spreading fastes in the world. Countries that embrace Islam build their societies based entirely on the basic laws of Islam and reject the materialism and way of life of the technologically more advance nations.

The United Nations General Assembly adopted–the Universal Declaration of Human Rights on December 1948. Islamic countries like Saudi Arabia, Iran, and Pakistan "criticized often the U.D.O.H.R. for its perceived failure to take into account the cultural and religious content of non-Western countries. In 1981 the Iranian representative to the United Nations, Said Rajaie-Khorassani, stated that the U.D.O.H.R. was a secular understanding of the Judeo-Christian tradition which could not be implemented by Muslims without trespassing the Islamic law." For this reason, they created the Organization of the Islamic Conference. The OIC supports the Cairo Declaration on Human Rights in Islam.

After the brutal, fanatical 9/11 attack, which was followed later by the terrorists attack in Madrid, President George W. Bush decided that it was better to fight the terrorists in their own territory than in the United States. The best option, he thought, was to "grab the terrorist bull's horns" in the Middle East and break its neck. Hence the invasion and military occupation of Iraq. So far it hasn't happen that way, unfortunately.

Islam, which means "Submission to God," was created by an Arabian man, Mohammed (569=–632). He had come to profess that there was one God and that he was his prophet. His thoughts were set forth in the Koran. Islam was taken with enthusiasm and devotion by many Arab people. Besides a religion, it also became a political ideology. Muslim armies began a war of conquest and spread Islam as far as India and China. Islam also presented a serious challenge to Christian Europe in AD 641. Eventually the Muslims conquered parts of Africa, Spain and parts of France. The Muslims made very important contributions to civilization through their agricultural methods, their commercial, banking, and credit systems and their knowledge of physics, chemistry, mathematics and particularly medicine. They set an example of religious tolerance by permitting other religious groups like Christians and Jews (years 1037, 1085).

Today the most important Islamic nations are the Kingdom of Saudi Arabia, the Islamic Republic of Islam, and the Islamic Republic of Pakistan which has had nuclear weapons since 1998, the Kingdom of Malaysia, the Republic of Indonesia, and the Republic of Sudan among others.

Since its beginning in Greece, Western civilization has created new forms of political institutions that were opposed to ancient Oriental despotism. The emergence of new political institutions where religious dogma prevails absolutely in a nation represent a new challenge to Western political philosophy. Is the world moving toward a new form of theocracy? Is the separation of the state and religion obsolete or at least in discredit? Is the new religious dogmatic state a change for the better or for the worse? When Pope Benedict XVI spoke to the General Assembly of the United Nations about human rights not every nation agreed with him for religious reasons.

Monday, May 19, 2008

Chess in Havana =May 2008

The forty-fourth international chess tournament Capablanca in Memoriam was held in Havana from May 7 to May 18. Several grandmasters from different countries participated in this tournament which has been held for at least forty-five years. Dutch grand master and European champion Sergei Tiviakov is among the participants as are grandmasters Radoslaw Wojtaszek from Poland, Faruk Amonotov from Tajikistan, Igor Khenkin from Germany, and Lenier Dominguez Perez and Lazaro Bruzon from Cuba. Many other grand masters have participated in previous Capablanca in Memoriam tournaments, such as Vasily Smislov whogave me the honor of his autograph in the "Habana Libre" hotel in 1962. Grandmasters Boris Spassky, Mikhail Tal, and Bobby Fischer were also there.

Jose Raul Capablanca was born in Havana, Cuba, in November 1888 and died in New York City in March 1942. He had two children with his first wife Gloria, but they later divorced. He remarried in 1937. He met his second wife, a beautiful Russian émigré named Olga Choubaroff, in New York. Their marriage was a happy one and lasted until his death of a stroke at the Manhattan Chess Club in New York City at fifty-three years old.

The pictures of the Fort Morro, the city of Havana, and the tournament were taken by Sergei Tiviakov who represented the Netherlands in this tournament. Mr. Tiviakov has also proved to be an excellent photographer. Credits should also be given to ChessBase News, Spanish News page, and Ms. Nadja Woisin for her Spanish text.

National News

Senator Barack Obama is already aiming his attacks at Senator John McCain by linking him to President George W. Bush. The real battle for the presidential elections is already taking shape.

Monday, May 26, 2008

The Energy Crisis and the Economy

Wall Street stocks fell sharply again in the week ending May 23. Investors are worried that consumers "will cut back spending and this will hurt the overall economy." Consumers are already paying very high gasoline prices and since consumers account for more than two-thirds of the U.S. economic activity their reluctance to spend money will have a negative effect in the economy.

Oil prices closed at $130.81 a barrel last Thursday. The executives of Shell Oil Co., Chevron Corp., Conoco Phillips, BP America and Exxon Mobil were in a hearing on Capitol Hill on Thursday. Representative Steve Cohen, Democrat of Tennessee and member of the House Judiciary Committee, told them. "You are all gouging the American public, and it needs to stop." The Ford Motor Corporation will reduce vehicle production from now on and will be unable to reach profitability in 2009. Rising gasoline prices are having a negative effect on Ford Motor Company's sales.

In Europe the airline Air France-KLM, the biggest on that continent, "warned of a profound reshaping of the world airline industry caused by what is called the "explosion" in the price of oil."

There are reports that suggest that world oil supplies may not be able to keep up with future demands. This news is motivating European countries like Italy, Holland, Belgium, Sweden, and Germany to build nuclear energy plants. However, as some critics point out, new nuclear plants take twenty years to build and there is also the problem of how to dispose of nuclear waste.

Monday, June 2, 2008

South Beach =Summer 2008

Famed Italian designer Gianni Versace's Casa Casuarina is an imitation of a sixteenth century palazzo that resembles the home of Diego Columbus, son of Christopher Columbus and governor of Hispaniola in Santo Domingo, Dominican Republic.

Ocean Drive is a street with many fine restaurants and with hotels facing the beaches that are constantly washed by the Atlantic Ocean.

For Floridians summer means that the hurricane season is back. It is the time of the year when they begin checking weather forecasts often, and maybe also checking a crystal ball to see the future.

Oil Crisis Shaking the World

There are protests across Europe by fishermen, farmers, and haulers in response to rocketing fuel prices. Fishermen in Spain, Portugal, and Italy went on a one-day strike and blocking ports. The Bulgarian government has been asked "to control speculative hikes in the price of diesel."

There have been reactions to the oil price explosion in other parts of the world as well. Indonesia, Taiwan and India have taken measures in order to deal with this crisis. In South America, however, some countries have fared better.

In the United States motorists drove eleven billion fewer miles in March than the prior year, according to the transportation department. Everybody is watching Wall Street. As reported by France 24, "The US Commodity Futures Trading Commission has launched a probe into possible price-fixing on America oil markets".

Thursday, June 5, 2008

Chess and the Seventh Art

Chess has been a favorite theme in movies for a long time. The struggles of human life are sometimes related to the conflicts that occur on the chessboard. An obsession with the game by an immature person may create a human drama. This was the case in the novel *The Luzhin Defence*, by Vladimir Nabokov. The movie version of Nabokov's novel was released in 2001.

There is a painting from 1480 in a medieval church in Taby, north of Stockholm that depicts a man playing chess with a skeletal Death. This painting inspired Ingmar Bergman to write his play *Wood Painting* which he later adapted into his movie *The Seventh Seal*.

Ingmar Bergman's film *The Seventh Seal*, 1958, is about a knight, Antonius Block, who returns with his squire, Jons, from the Crusades. He is going back to his castle in Sweden where his wife, Landgre, has been waiting for him for ten years. These are the Dark Ages and the Black Plague is devastating Europe. Death arrives to take the knight and his squire away but Block tries to convince Death to give him another chance. He proposes that he and Death should play a game of chess. If he loses he will let Death take him away but if he wins Death must promise to stay away. Death find this amusing because he knows he never loses at anything. The movie is based on a short play by Bergman and was a low-budget production. It won the Special Jury Prize at the Cannes Film Festival in 1957, and it made Bergman a celebrity.

Searching for Bobby Fischer is not a movie about chess, but about the relationship of a child chess prodigy and his parents. It is based on the true story of Josh Waitzkin. In the movie *Casablanca*, 1942, Humphrey Bogart plays a game of chess. He was considered to be a strong player in real life.

Monday, June 9, 2008

National News

Senator Barack Obama has been nominated as the Democratic presidential candidate. He is the first Afro-American presidential candidate in America history. Senator Obama appeared in a photo with his wife Michelle in St. Paul, Minnesota.

In other news Senator Hillary R. Clinton ended her campaign for the Democratic nomination and asked her supporters to endorse Senator Obama. We don't know at this time if she would like to be the vice-presidential candidate on a ticket with Senator Obama.

South Florida News

Evictions in South Florida

The present economic crisis in the United States is affecting not only people living below the poverty level but also middle-class families.

Police Officer Albert Fernandez, of the Miami-Dade County Police Department, has been serving eviction papers to people for ten years. He said that never before has he served eviction papers as he does now. "People of all walks of life are getting evicted," he said.

International News

Hugo Chavez —Venezuela, South America.

Mr. Hugo Chavez, president of Venezuela, apparently has been caught helping the Colombian Marxist guerrilla organization FARC. Computer files captured during a Colombian Army raid of a FARC camp in Ecuador has proved his complicity in trying to overthrow the Colombian government. The authenticity of the computer files was confirmed by Interpol. Chavez denies the charges. President Chavez is also tightening his grip on the Venezuelan people by using "his decree powers to carry out a major overhaul of this country's intelligence agencies, provoking a fierce backlash here (Caracas, Venezuela) from Human Rights groups and legal scholars...." The new measures taken by President Chavez are "a step toward the creation of a society of informers." "This is purely Cuban-style policy, says legislator Mr. Juan Jose Molina."

Economy

The New York Times, Friday, June 6, 2008

The Dow Jones Industrial Average fell about 400 points driven by economic concerns and by oil prices that soared to near $140 a barrel.

Quotations of the Day

"It has been said that man is a rational animal. All my life I have been searching for evidence which could support this."

Bertrand Russell

Monday, June 16, 2008

The Durability of the Book

Books can last for many years if kept in a controlled-climate. That's not the case with electronic data-storage devices like floppy disks, videotapes, and hard disks. The relatively short life of electronic storage parts is a fact. A well preserved book may last four hundred years but electronic storage devices will last only a fraction of that time. Magnetic fields, oxidation and material decay shorten their lives rapidly. Also technology is changing continuously. Floppy disks are seldom used today, and videotapes are already being displaced by digital CD's.

Libraries are also having problems with technology. Their budgets for new technologies have risen at least 80 percent. They purchase equipment and software that in the near future will have to be replaced with new versions. The electronic archives are certainly not a safe place for saving our videos and pictures for the long term. And "librarians and archivists warn that we're losing vast amounts of important scientific and historical material because of disintegration or obsolescence." Under optimal storage conditions, audiotapes and videotapes will last ten years, newspapers twenty years, CD-ROMs fifty years, archival-quality microfilm two-hundred years, and archival-quality paper five hundred years.

PART THREE
Summer 2008

Monday, June 30, 2008

The Economy

Last Thursday, June 26, the stock market on Wall Street dived 358 points after receiving a disappointing report about the biggest brokerage firms.

On Friday oil prices continued to climb to new highs and on Wall Street the Dow fell a little again after yesterday tumble.

Use and Abuse of Prescriptions Drugs

The Florida Department of Law Enforcement has found in a recent study that there is an increasingly serious problem with prescription drug abuse. There are many ways in the state of Florida to get prescriptions drugs: from health care providers, by doctor shopping, or by theft of drug shipments. The federal Drug Enforcement Administration in similar studies has found that nearly seven million Americans are misusing prescribed medications, and this is an increase of 80 percent in the last six years. Drugs like Valium and Xanax caused 743 deaths. Alcohol caused 466 deaths fewer than those caused by cocaine which caused 843 deaths.

The Florida Medical Examiners Commission has found that the rate of deaths caused by prescribed medications was three times higher than the rate of deaths caused by all illicit drugs combined. The well publicized case of Anna Nicole Smith is an example of this problem. She died of an accidental prescription drug overdose. Prescription drug abuse has reached epidemic proportions.

Today's Quotation

"For a list of all the ways technology has failed to improve the quality of life, please press three."

Alice Kahn

Tuesday, July 8, 2008

Hurricane Season in the Atlantic Ocean and Caribbean Sea

Hurricane Bertha is the first hurricane of the 2008 season. It is currently located 975 miles (1570 km.) southeast of Bermuda, in the Atlantic. It has been downgraded from category 3 to category 2. So far it doesn't represent any danger to land.

The deadliest hurricanes in U.S. history struck Galveston, Texas, in 1900, Florida in 1928 and the Florida Keys in 1935. Other devastating hurricanes were Hurricane Audrey in 1957 and hurricane Katrina in 2005.

National News

Senator Barack Obama assured that his political position has not changed at all. Speaking in Powder Springs, Georgia, he dismissed such publications absurd, as reported by the *Washington Post*.

Music

The Beatles are celebrating the anniversary of their appearance in the *Ed Sullivan Show* forty-four years ago. Ringo Starr who was the drummer of the band is on tour in Chicago. To commemorate this anniversary, the band members are going to throw a party with the theme Peace and Love.

CNN News.

Monday, July 14, 2008

Obedience and the Stanley Milgram Experiments

Among the different schools of thoughts in psychology there are two that can be related to Stanley Milgram's obedience studies: the genetics psychology school which states that human behavior is determined by heredity and the stimulus-response (behaviorist) school which says that behavior is formed by experience and learning that is, by the environment in which we are raised which includes our families and society.

Until the end of last century psychology was mainly concerned with the individual. Further research has concluded that human character is not very stable.

Professor Stanley Milgram was troubled by the genocide committed by Hitler's government in Germany in World War II. Millions of Jews and other undesirable people such as Gypsies were sent to extermination camps in a program of ethnic cleansing. Milgram was distressed because many ordinary people of different cultural and social backgrounds remained indifferent to this genocide and others participated in the slaughter. For this reason Milgram devised a series of experiments at Yale University in Connecticut in the 1960's to test individual behavior. The experiments are known as the Stanley Milgram shock experiments.

A fake voltage machine was made and forty men of all ages and occupations were asked to participate in "an important study of learning." Each participant was placed at the controls of the machine, a dial labeled with voltages, that supposedly delivered electric shocks to a "learner" that was supposed to master an assignment. (The learner was really an actor and accomplice of the experimenter a scientist and a figure of authority in this case.) Every time that the learner made a mistake the participant had to shock him. If the participant hesitated the experimenter pressured him by saying "It is absolutely essential that you continue," and, "You have no other choice; you *must* go on." The intensity of the (fake) shocks went from slight (15 to 60 volts) to severe (as high as 450 volts). At one point the learner began hitting the wall to indicate distress and one-third of the participants dropped out. The others two-thirds continued to deliver shocks, all the way to what was labeled the danger zone 450 volts.

Milgram concluded that the participants in his obedience experiments "were influenced by the setting =a laboratory designed for the advancement of science and also they were impressed by the authority of the scientist who was pressing them to continue.

This experiment showed that "where the location or social environment and people with authority can influence behavior is the main concern of *Social Psychology*. ...—. We cannot fully understand individuals by studying them in isolation (*Gestalt Psychology*)."

Monday, July 21, 2008

Presidential Elections in the United States

Senator Barack Obama will face a big hurdle in the race for the White House. Most white Americans believe that he is a demagogue rather than a politician with honest intentions to solve the problems of the nation. His comments in the past that many white blue collar workers like "to cling to guns and the Bible" have created resentment among them. They also dislike his wife Michelle and only 24 percent would like to see her as the first lady. There are white people that just don't want blacks being on the top of the political power. Only 37 percent of white voters support Senator Obama while 46 percent support Senator McCain.

Among black voters the picture is different as 89 percent of African-Americans support Senator Obama. Hispanics that strongly supported Senator Hillary Clinton probably will favor Senator Obama this time.

Since population of the United States is 82 percent white and only 13 percent black* Senator Obama will have to use his best abilities as a politician to unite the American people and persuade them to vote for political issues and not for the color of his skin.

* *The World Almanac and Book of Facts* =2008

Economy

There is a pessimistic feeling about the U.S. economy in some circles of the government. President Bush in an unscheduled news conference last Tuesday recognized that the economy is going through hard times. However he emphasized that "the economy continues growing, consumers are spending, businesses are investing, exports continue increasing and American productivity remains strong."

Mr. Ben S. Bernanke, chairman of the Federal Reserve, testifying before the Senate Banking Committee, gave a more bleak picture of the economy.

Latin America: Cuba

President Raul Castro has lately been making cosmetic political changes in Cuba. He has allowed the sales of cell phones and computers which a large majority of Cubans cannot afford to buy. Besides, access to the Internet is restricted to only a few people.

The skyrocketing of food prices worldwide has hit Cuba very hard. This has made Mr. Castro's government reconsider some Marxist economic principles established. The Cuban government is the largest landowner on the island and food production by farmers working for the state is sluggish. Consequently reform is on the way to give plots to private farmers in order to boost food production. The new plan was officially announced last Friday, July 18. But for the Cuban people who have lived with food rationing cards for the last fifty years, that won't mean much.

Monday, July 28, 2008

U.S. Presidential Race: The Hare and The Tortoise

Senator Barack Obama has finished his tour of the Middle East and western Europe. In Israel he was received warmly by President Shimon Peres. The two men met later. In Berlin Senator Obama was cheered by a crowd of at least two hundred thousand people, most of them under forty, that stretched for nearly a mile. He addressed them in the park Tiergarten not too far from the Brandenburg Gate where Presidents John F. Kennedy and Ronald Reagan spoke. Western Europe and America's relations have been damaged by President George W. Bush's remarks about the "old Europe" and global warming issues, and Senator Obama assured the crowd that if he's elected president of the United States, he will bring western Europe and America together again. He also spoke about the battle against terrorism in Afghanistan. He made a brief stop in Paris where he was received by French President Nicolas Sarkozy. The men commented that they are both children of immigrants and now have political careers. The French people are beginning to catch "Obamamania." Senator Obama continued his international trip in Great Britain.

Senator John McCain's political campaign has been moving at a slower but steady pace. Polls released recently showed that he's gaining in several swing states like Michigan, Wisconsin, and Minnesota. He may also already have a lead in Colorado. His political base is indeed very solid.

Monday, August 4, 2008

Political Prisoners in Cuba and Carnival in Havana Streets

The people of Havana are getting ready for this year's carnivals, as Ms. Yoani Sanchez reports from that city in her well known blog Generation Y. It will be a nice change for a few days of the tedious and politically suffocating days of the rest of the year. News of the cult of personality of the terminally ill Fidel Castro will be replaced by the performance of the delightful figures of the conga dancers shaking their hips. Once the conga groups raise their lampposts, strike the bongos and begin to move, the crowd will follow them step by step. And the crowd may chant something like "One, two and three, great is the conga beat!"…. One, two and three, great is the conga beat!" It's intoxicating. The tourists may be astonished to find such joy and the ruling Cuban Communist Mandarins will be proud of such success.

Last April 22 ten members of the Cuban human rights group Ladies in White were grabbed by the police when they tried to deliver a letter to officials in Havana seeking release of their husbands or relatives that were in jail for political reasons. Other group of women also were arrested for the same reason. Political prisoner Juan Carlos Herrera Acosta, an opposition journalist, is on a hunger strike. Other political prisoners, Alfredo Rodolfo Dominguez Batista, Orlando Zapata Tamayo, and Luis Mariano Delis Utria are joining Herrera in his protest. Herrera is in very bad health. These are just a few names of a large population of political prisoners. Most Cubans are not informed about these incidents and those who do know something keep themselves very quiet for fear of reprisal by the government.

The Cuban Communists Mandarins will keep telling under developed countries of the success of the Revolution. And people in these countries may believe their propaganda.

In the meantime "Liborio" (the Cuban people) is sitting at the door of his house waiting to see pass by the corpse of his enemy.

Wednesday, August 13, 2008

The Olympic Games

The Olympic Games originated in Olympia, Greece, in 776 BC. The International Olympic Committee was created in 1894 by the French aristocrat Pierre Fredy, Baron de Couberth. The Olympic Games in Beijing, China, this year will include 302 events in 28 sports.

Beijing 2008 Summer Olympic Games

The colorful and lavish 2008 Summer Olympic Games in Beijing, China, will be carried out from August 8 to August 24. Former IOC president Juan Antonio Samaranch said that these games will be "the best in Olympic history." The Chinese government has spent heavily on these Olympic Games in order to show the world that China is a world power in athleticism.

During the opening ceremonies on August 8 the crowd heard the sound of heavy footsteps in the Bird's Nest when performers marched to the National Stadium, and they saw huge burning footprints across the sky.

The artistic performances of the opening ceremonies were divided in two parts. The first part, "Brilliant Civilization," showed the past five thousand years of Chinese civilization, and the second half, "Glorious Era," showed more recent history.

Monday, August 25, 2008

The Economy, Hurricanes, and Olympic Games

The Economy

Inflation has increased to a level not seen since 1991. The Labor Department has reported that the cost of living is very much exceeding the salaries of most Americans. Food and gasoline costs are a major contribution to the economic squeeze that is affecting the American people.

Producer prices jumped 1.2 percent in July. The *New York Times* reports that the "inflation rate at the wholesale level is running at the fastest annual pace since 1981, .—.... while the number of new houses and apartments .—.... slumped to their lowest level in 17 years, according to new government statistics."

Hurricanes

Tropical storm Fay has set a (non-Olympic) record with four landfalls in the peninsula of Florida. Eleven people have been killed and thousands of homes and businesses have been inundated with flood waters this week. A slow-moving tropical storm can be as deadly as a hurricane.

The 2008 Olympic Games in Beijing

Spectacular fireworks and lavish choreography closed the 2008 Olympic Games in Beijing. More than ninety thousand people in National Stadium watched the fireworks. With these games, China has presented itself as a world superpower in athletics. London, Great Britain, will be the host of the 2012 Summer Games. China has spent more than forty billion dollars on this Summer Olympic Games.

The US men's basketball team won the gold medal beating Spain118 to 107.

In the medal standings China is in first place with fifty-one gold medals, the United States is in second place with thirty-six gold medals, Russia is in third place with twenty-three gold medals, Great Britain is in fourth place with nineteen gold medals, and Germany in fifth place with sixteen gold medals.

Monday, September 1, 2008

Labor Day =US Presidential Candidates = Weather

Presidential Elections in the United States = November 4, 2008:

Monday, September 1, is Labor Day so most Americans are enjoying a long weekend. They also know now who the candidates for both major political parties are for the next presidential elections.

Senator John McCain has just announced his running mate for vice=president Mrs. Sarah Palin who is governor of Alaska.

Senator Barack Obama was nominated as his party's candidate by a unanimous vote. He has made history by becoming the first Afro-American to become nominee for president of this republic. He has chosen Senator Joseph R. Biden, Jr., of Delaware as his vice-president. Senator Biden has a deep knowledge of foreign policy which Mr. Obama lacks.

Hurricane Season

Two tropical storms, Gustav and Hanna, are in this region.

Gustav has already killed sixty-seven people in Haiti and the Dominican Republic and has slashed Jamaica. It is expected to head toward the US Gulf Coast. Louisiana is on high alert.

Hanna is north of Cuba, in the Atlantic Ocean, and its path at this time is unpredictable.

Monday, September 8, 2008

US Presidential Race, the Economy and Hurricanes

National Politics
The Race for the White House.

The election for the next president of the United States will be held on November 4.

For the Republican party the candidate is Mr. John McCain and for the Democratic party the candidate is Mr. Barack Obama. Both candidates have told the American people that changes are necessary in order to move this country forward again. However they have different strategies for achieving these changes. The economy is stagnant, unemployment is high by US standards and the American people have the worst health care protection of all industrialized countries in the Western world.

The race for the White House has taken off between the Tortoise (Mr. McCain), and the Hare (Mr. Obama).-

The Economy

The unemployment rate in the United States went up to 6.1 percent in August, which is the highest in five years. Also the American economy lost eighty-four thousand private no farms jobs in August alone. The poor state of the American economy has hit world financial markets hard and US and European shares have fallen sharply. Also rumors of hedge fund failures have contributed to the fall of the stock markets.

The Hurricane Season

The Atlantic basin is very active with several tropical storms at the present time. A train of three tropical storms are keeping the Caribbean islands inhabitants on edge. The peninsula of Florida is being caught in the cross-fire of tropical storms. It is true that September is always the peak of hurricane activity but this year has been worse than others.

Lake Okeechobee, which is located in the center of Florida, is almost full of water from the rain that Fay brought. The water level as of September 5 is 14.78 feet. The Army Corps of Engineers said last Tuesday, September 2, that they will be draining the lake to begin slowing "the lake's record-setting rise and lowering the potential risk to its aging levee." This big lake is a drinking water source for many communities around it.

Tuesday, September 16, 2008

The 9/11 Terrorist Attack = The Wrath of Mother Nature

The Seventh Anniversary of 9/11 Terrorist Attacks

Last Thursday was the seventh anniversary of the September 11 attacks by terrorists on New York's World Trade Center and the Pentagon. I was particularly sensitive about the attack on the World Trade Center because I am quite familiar with downtown Manhattan. I worked for several years in that area.

In 1966 I worked as banking clerk in Exchange Place. I later worked in a securities firm on Pine Street, and even later in another financial corporation on 67 Broad Street as an accounting clerk. At lunch-time I always went out for a walk and I enjoyed these strolls through the always busy streets of downtown Manhattan. My strolls took me down Broad Street, Wall Street, Nassau Street, Rector Street, Trinity Church, and Battery Park. In 1971 I moved with my family to Miami. That was also a very good year.

The Wrath of Mother Nature

Hurricanes Gustav and Ike have left a trail of destruction and misery in the Caribbean nations of the Dominican Republic, Haiti and Cuba. Haiti in particular has had many deaths because it is a very poor country with very few resources of its own. In Cuba the damage caused by Ike are estimated to be between three and four billion dollars, according to the United Nations. There have been extensive damages to homes, buildings, agriculture and power infrastructures. Hurricane Ike has also hit Texas very hard and there are nearly three million people without electricity in the Houston area. Getting rescue to people in Galveston is extremely difficult.

Economy

Powerful financial institutions on Wall Street are in deep economic crisis. Lehman Brothers filed for bankruptcy protection and Merril

Lynch agreed to sell itself to Bank of America for fifty billion dollars. This crisis in the United States is shaking the stock markets in the rest of the world.

PART FOUR
Autumn 2008

Monday, September 22, 2008

September 15 Wall Street Collapsed!

On September 15 the world financial markets were shaken after receiving bad news from Wall Street. The outstanding securities firm Lehman Brothers filed for bankruptcy protection and Merril Lynch sold itself to Bank of America for fifty billion dollars. Furthermore American International Group (AIG), the largest insurance company in the world, has reported huge losses due to the credit crisis. The Dow Jones Industrial Average fell more than 500 points on Monday due to investor reactions to this news.

In the mid 90's U.S. banks began giving mortgages to high-risk borrowers. These high-risk mortgages were then transformed into mortgage backed securities (MBSs) that could be exchanged on stock markets. When home owners were unable to pay their mortgages companies holding these securities went bankrupt. Eventually the MBSs were worthless and caused Bear Stearns to collapse and a credit crunch because banks refuse to lend money.

This financial crisis is also the result of the economic philosophy of the free market upheld by the Bush administration. In this system, bankers, lenders, and insurers have nearly a free hand to make their financial transactions with very few restrictions. Laissez-faire economic policies, such as Milton Friedman's monetarism are inadequate. The government has to regulate and supervise the business operations of financial executives. Otherwise the unscrupulous greed of several powerful individuals in the financial world will harm the common welfare of the people.

Monday, October 6, 2008

Writing and Democracy

1982

The Ability to Write A Root of Democracy

Writing has always been one of the pillars of democracy.

In 1787 the Constitution of the United States was created and was accepted by the delegates of all thirteen states in 1789. It originated a new political system, the republic, which was different from the European political systems at the time. In Europe by the end of the nineteenth century the press was so important to creating political public opinions that it was called the Fourth Estate.

In literature we have the novella *One Day in the Life of Ivan Denisovich* by Nobel laureate Alexander Solzhenitsyn, published in Russian in 1962. Solzhenitsyn exposed in this story the cruelty of Stalin's forced-labor camps.

Tuesday, October 14, 2008

Dark Week for Wall Street October 10, 2008

Monday, October 13, 2008. Light at the End of the Tunnel?

Stocks rallied Monday afternoon on Wall Street by 11 percent and the Dow Jones Industrial Average gained 936 points breaking 9,100. Investors are hoping that the worst of the credit crisis is over.

European leaders of the biggest economies announced massive bank bailouts this morning. They have been forced into action by the biggest financial crisis in the world since the Great Depression. German Chancellor Merkel said that the German government will provide $536.7 billion in guarantees for banks. French President Sarkozy said that his government will spend up to $490 billion on its bank rescue plan, and Spanish Prime Minister Zapatero said that his government will set aside up to $134 billion for inter=bank loans. The United Kingdom will give up to $63 billion as part of its the rescue plan.

Last Friday U.S. stocks plunged 4.7 percent in the afternoon with the Dow down 403 points. It was another day of sharp swings in a week of large sell-offs. The major stock markets in Europe and Asia also declined Friday due to uncertainty about global financial problems and the inability of world political leaders to find a satisfactory solution. In India industrial grow slowed down, in Sweden Volvo laid off thousands of employees and in Japan small businesses went into bankruptcy. Around the world fears of a recession have spread.

Jerry Batstone of London's Charles Stanley brokerage firm said that the present rescue plans of the major economic world powers have averted a global economic depression but would not save it from a recession. Mr. Batstone added that "the recession is likely to be long and it's likely to be deep."

Thursday, November 6, 2008

Barack H. Obama President of the United States of America

Barack H. Obama was elected as the forty-fourth president of the United States of America. He is forty-seven years old and a first term senator from Illinois. He's a charismatic politician and an excellent orator. Senator Obama told a huge crowd in Chicago "If there is anyone out there who still doubts that America is a place where all things are possible, who still wonders if the dream of our founders is alive in our times, who still questions the power of our democracy, tonight is your answer."

The Economy

The Dow fell more than 400 points for a second day. Shares on Wall Street plunged for a second day on Thursday among weak sales reports from retailers. Concerns about the economy and weak spending sent the major stock exchanges down more than 4 percent Thursday, including the Dow Jones Industrial Average, which tumbled more than 443 points. The broader Standard & Poor's 500-stock index fell 5 percent.

Monday, November 10, 2008

The Wall Street Crash and The Black Swan Theory

In the ancient Western world it was assumed that all swans were white. Therefore in philosophical discussions the term "black swan" indicated the improbable.

Mr. Nassim Nicholas Taleb, an epistemologist and specialist in financial derivatives, wrote the book *The Black Swan* in 2007. It refers to unpredictable events with very strong consequences. His opinions in this book are presented as a conjecture. He says that "globalization created interlocking fragility.... ... We have never lived before under the threat of a global collapse.... ... Scientists working for the government-sponsored institution Fannie Mae said that the risks explained by Mr. Taleb were 'unlikely'."

Weather

Hurricane Paloma slammed the province of Camaguey, on the southern coast of Cuba destroying hundreds of homes. This is the third hurricane hitting the island in this hurricane season. The other two were Gustav and Ike.

Economy

Another 240,000 jobs were lost in the United States in October. Since consumers have very little cash they are spending very little and this is having a negative effect in the economy.

The economy is sliding deeper into a recession, some economists believe.

Tuesday, November 18, 2008

Twenty-fifth Miami Book Fair International

Last Saturday I visited the Miami Book Fair at Miami Dade College's Wolfson Campus, a few blocks from downtown Miami. The afternoon was cool and nice. The attendees moved in all directions stopping at the booths to browse the books and maybe purchase them.

There were also interesting presentations by local journalists like Messrs. Carl Hiassen and Jorge Ramos as well by international journalists and writers. Hollywood sent us Mr. George Hamilton who was promoting his book *Don't Mind If I Do*.

It was another extraordinary cultural event brought to us by Miami Dade College with the support of Miami-Dade County.

Quote of the Day

"Nobody realizes that some people expend tremendous energy merely to be normal."
Albert Camus

National News = Economy

Activity on Wall Street declined again Tuesday, November 18, as investors saw a volatile market reacting to a flow of weak economic data.

These are very hard times for Detroit automakers. Ford and General Motors are selling their investments in Mazda Motor Corp. and Suzuki Motor Corp. to raise cash. It's a futile action in a race against bankruptcy. GM is spending its cash reserves at a rate of two billion dollars a month.

International News

The biggest tanker ever sized by pirates, the *Sirius Star*, is anchored off the Somali coast. The twenty-five-member crew of the Saudi oil tanker is safe. The ship is carrying two million barrels of oil.

Pirates have also seized a cargo ship in the Gulf of Aden. Pirate attacks have increased 100 percent off the coast of Somalia.

Sunday, November 23, 2008

Ernest Hemingway in Havana

In August 1965 I visited Hemingway's house Finca Vigia in the town of Cojimar, Havana. The Cuban Communist government had already made the house into a museum of the late American writer's life. There were still a few cats in the house's surroundings. The guide took us inside the house and we could see bookcases and shelves in different rooms containing many books.

After the Second World War Hemingway came back to his home in Havana. He wrote the novella *The Old Man and the Sea* which was published in 1952. In 1953 he received the Pulitzer Prize in fiction for this work and in 1954 he won the Nobel Prize for Literature.

The Old Man and the Sea is about an old Cuban fisherman, Santiago, who has spent eighty-four days in the Gulf of Mexico without a catch. On the eighty-fifth day he catches a gigantic marlin. He fights the fish for two days until he is able to harpoon it. Soon sharks showed up and begin eating parts of the marlin, Santiago tries to kill them but his knife breaks. On his way back to land the sharks devour all of the marlin except its head. Once Santiago arrives in the harbor, other fishermen wonder at the size of the skeleton and Santiago feels victorious.

This story has been interpreted "as an allegory of man's inevitable defeat in the struggle with existence; in spite of defeat, however, man can fight with dignity, courage, and stoicism."

Sunday, December 14, 2008

Tour of the City of St. Augustine, Florida

This tour of St. Augustine was a pilgrimage sponsored by the Father Felix Varela Foundation of the Shrine of Our Lady of Charity (Catholic church) in Miami. It was directed and supervised by the benevolent Monsignor Agustin Roman, with the help of Rev. Deacon Manolo Perez. I would like to thank Dr. Rafael B. Abislaiman for the important information he gave the tour group about Father Felix Varela's life in St. Augustine. Dr. Rafael Abislaiman's book *Pilgrimaging to San Agustin* is very valuable as a source of information. My special thanks also go to Mrs. Margarita Miranda who brought me back to my home Sunday night.

On Saturday at 6:30 AM we left Miami on a pilgrimage to the city of St. Augustine where the Cuban priest and patriot Father Felix Varela lived from 1850 to 1853. He died on February 25, 1853 and was buried in the Tolomato cemetery. While living in Cuba under Spanish rule, he was a professor at the Seminary College of San Carlos which was "the most important education center in colonial Cuba." He taught the Cubans "to think." Eventually he had to go into exile.

We arrived in St. Augustine Saturday afternoon and visited Tolomato cemetery, where Monsignor Agustin Roman gave us some interesting historical details. We left St. Augustine on Sunday at 4:30 PM. It was a very pleasant and instructive tour.

St. Augustine is a historical city in the United States. Spain sent two expeditions to Florida in 1513 and 1565 that were a failure. However King Philip II considered Florida a very important territory for protecting the Spanish fleet's treasures from Mexico and South America in its voyage back to Spain. For this reason he gave the assignment to colonize Florida to Captain Pedro Menendez de Aviles. The fleet commanded by Captain Aviles arrived on September 8, 1565 at a place just north of Cape Canaveral and founded a settlement named St. Augustine. It became the first European city in North America.

After the Seven Years' War Florida became part of the British Empire.

Saturday, December 20, 2008

Tennessee Williams and His Last Play

Tennessee Williams is considered to be the most important American dramatist of the post-World War II era. His plays show "primitive violence a quality he believes lurks beneath the surface of modern life." He lived for thirty years in Key West. On January 5, 1979, his gardener was murdered. After that he was attacked twice in the streets, and one evening some children went to the doorstep of his home and yelled to this great American playwright "Come on out, faggot!" He moved later to New York where he died in a hotel room in 1983 at the age of seventy-one.

The New World Festival of The Arts, a three-week celebration of the arts, was presented in June 1982 in Dade County. As part of this festival the Gusman Cultural Center in downtown Miami showed Tennessee Williams's last play, *A House Not Meant to Stand*. I had the privilege to see this play Thursday, June 17, 1982, at 2:30 PM

A House Not Meant to Stand is not among the best plays of Tennessee Williams although one critic said "it is probably the best thing the playwright has written since Small Craft Warnings, a decade ago." Williams called this dark comedy a "Southern Gothic spook sonata."

The play is about Cornelius and his wife Bella McCorkle from Pascagoula, Mississippi. They have three children. Their oldest child, a gay man, has just died. Their daughter is in an insane asylum, and their youngest child, Charlie is upstairs having sex with his girlfriend. This family along with its three spectral children is falling apart.

PART FIVE
Winter 2009

Saturday, January 17, 2009

US Economy and World Affairs

Economy

The U. S. lost 524,000 jobs in December, and 7.2 percent of the labor forced is unemployed. This is a sixteen-year high. There are 11.1 millions unemployed workers so far which is nearly 50 percent more than the number when the recession started last year. Most economists believe that the recession will continue in 2009.

Citigroup posted a $8.29 billion loss and will split the company into two separate businesses, Citicorp and Citi Holdings, as reported January 16. Bank of America will receive $20 billion as a capital injection from the government.

In Japan Honda is going to eliminate 3,100 jobs. In Europe markets fell due to Asian losses. The price of oil dropped to $38 January 13 due to global recession.

National News

On January 15 a US Airways plane made an emergency water landing in the Hudson River in New York. Flight 1540 an Airbus 320 carrying 150 passengers and five crew members, was bound for Charlotte, North Carolina from New York's La Guardia Airport. All people on-board were rescued by New York rescue teams. Passengers suffered no serious injuries except one passenger, who had two broken legs. It seems that birds got into the plane's two engines and caused the accident. The National Transportation Safety Board is investigating this accident. The pilot of the plane, Captain Chesley B "Sully" Sullenberger III, and his copilot Jeff Skiles are hailed as heroes. New York Mayor Michael Bloomberg plans to present a Key to the City to the pilot.

International News

Middle East. Israel launched a military attack against Palestine to annihilate Hamas militiamen that have been firing rockets into Israel. More than one thousand Palestinians including children and women, have died in this war.

The Caribbean. Former President Fidel Castro's health is causing rumors again in Miami. The ailing Cuban Communist leader had surgery in 2006 and has retired from public life since then. He has given interviews only to dignitaries from friendly countries like Venezuela, China, and Brazil. Since he's already eighty-two years old and almost died during his surgery in 2006 his possibilities of living much longer are dimming. He has ruled longer than any other political leader in the world.

Monday, January 26, 2009

Barack Obama Forty-Fourth President of the United States

Barack Hussein Obama was sworn in as the forty-fourth president of the United States Tuesday, January 21, the day after the Dr. Martin Luther King Jr. Day. Dr. King dedicated his life to the improving of the social and political conditions of African=Americans. Because he is African American, Mr. Obama's election by the large majority of Americans has, without any doubt, historical significance.

Mr. Obama is facing very grave obstacles left by George W. Bush's administration: the world financial crisis and the wars in Iraq and Afghanistan.

More than 1.5 million Americans of all races and ages, enduring freezing conditions on Inauguration Day, came to the National Mall in Washington DC to welcome the new president. Let's extend to him our best wishes in his new tough job.